READING FOR THE CONTEMPORARY GUITARIST

Volume 4

©2022 Ian Robbins

All rights reserved. No part of this book may be reprinted or reproduced or utilized in any form or by any electronic, mechanical, or other means, now known or hereafter therein, including photocopying and recording, or in any information storage or retrieval system, without permission in writing from the publisher.

Trademark notice: Product or corporate names may be trademarks or registered trademarks, and are used only for identification and explanation without intent to infringe.

Library of Congress Cataloging-in-Publication Data
Name: Robbins, Ian Matthew, author.
Title: Reading for the Contemporary Guitarist Volume 4/ Ian Robbins
Identifiers: LCCN TXu2209262 | ISBN 9781732996885 (paperback) | ISBN 9781732996892

ISBN: 9781732996885 (paperback)
ISBN: 9781732996892 (ebook)

Table of Contents

CHAPTER 1: COMBINING POSITIONS I-X, TWO STRING HORIZONTAL READING, AND JAZZ SWING FEEL ... 3

- Wide Range Reading ... 3
- Two String Horizontal Reading ... 8
- Introduction to Jazz Swing Feel ... 11
- Assignment: ... 17

CHAPTER 2: INTRODUCTION TO POSITION XI, JAZZ SWING CONT., INTRODUCTION TO JAZZ COUNTERPOINT ... 19

- Position XI ... 19
- Jazz Swing Feel Continued ... 24
- Introduction to Jazz Counterpoint ... 29
- Assignment: ... 31

CHAPTER 3: POSITION XI CONT., JAZZ SWING FEEL SYNCOPATION CONT., AND INTRODUCTION TO ODD METER ... 33

- Jazz Swing Syncopation Continued ... 38
- Introduction to Odd Meter ... 42
- Assignment: ... 45
- Combining Positions X and XI ... 49
- Odd Meter Continued ... 51
- 16th Note Triplets ... 55
- Cumulative Review Exercises ... 58
- Assignment: ... 61
- Position XII ... 63
- Tied Eighth Note Triplet Syncopation Swing Exercises ... 69
- Jazz Chordal Reading Position VII ... 71
- Assignment: ... 75

CHAPTER 6: POSITION XII CONT., CHORDAL READING IN POSITION IX, INTRODUCTION TO MIXED METER, 32ND NOTE READING ... 77

- Chordal Reading Position IX ... 79
- Mixed Meter ... 81
- 32nd Note Reading ... 86
- Assignment: ... 91

CHAPTER 7: POSITION XII CONT., MIXED METER CONT., COMPREHENSIVE REVIEW EXERCISES ... 93

Position VII 8va Review 95
Mixed Meter Continued 98
Articulation Review Exercises 102
Assignment: 105

CHAPTER 8: INTRODUCTION TO POSITION XII 8VA, DOUBLE AND TRIPLE STOPS IN POSITION IX, JAZZ SYNCOPATION AND ODD METER REVIEW 107

Jazz Syncopation Review Exercises 112
Double and Triple Stop Reading 114
Odd Meter Reading Review 116
Assignment: 119

CHAPTER 9: HIGH REGISTER READING, DOUBLE STOP READING (HORIZONTAL APPROACH, AND MIXED METER REVIEW EXERCISES 121

High Ledger Line Reading 124
Double Stop Reading: Horizontal Approach 127
Mixed Meter Review Exercises 130
Assignment: 133

CHAPTER 10: POSITIONS I-XII COMBINED, HARMONY READING (HORIZONTAL APPROACH), ODD AND MIXED METER APPLIED READING 135

Positionless Reading 135
Harmony Reading (Horizontal Approach) 140
Odd and Mixed Meter Review Exercises 143
Practice Charts 146

Chapter 1: Combining Positions I-X, Two String Horizontal Reading, and Jazz Swing Feel

Wide Range Reading

The following exercises will contain ranges too large for just one position. Using the keys as your guide, try these examples using any combination of positions I-X:

1.1

1.2

1.3

1.16

1.17

1.18

1.19

1.20

1.21

Two String Horizontal Reading

Read the following examples horizontally using ONLY the indicated strings:

1st and 2nd Strings

1.22

2nd and 3rd Strings

1.23

3rd and 4th Strings

1.24

4th and 5th Strings

1.25

5th and 6th Strings

1.26

6th and 4th Strings

1.27

5th and 3rd Strings

1.28

4th and 2nd Strings

1.29

3rd and 1st Strings

1.30

Introduction to Jazz Swing Feel

A swing feel can be difficult to define because there can be some variance depending on the player and era of swing.

A heavy swing feel could be written as follows:

This would be more common in early swing genres.

An average swing feel could be notated thusly:

This looks identical to the shuffle feel, but the key difference is that swing would place more emphasis on the upbeat (or offbeat of the rhythm):

Some modern jazz players barely distinguish the difference in length of the two 8th notes.

Another aspect worth noting about the jazz swing feel is that the accent does not need to be equally loud on the off beats each time it is played and is often determined by the shape of the melodic line as to which notes should be accented more.

Tempo also plays a role in swing feel. The faster the tempo, the more even the 8th notes will begin to feel. At slower tempos the triplet feel will become much more pronounced.

Try following examples in any position you like using all three different swing feels:

1.31

1.32

*When an 8th note comes in after an 8th note rest, the swing should be treated the same on the second half of the beat as it would if it were two consecutive 8th notes.

1.33

1.34

* These two rhythms should be identical. You may see these written either way.

1.35

1.36

This page has been intentionally left blank

Assignment:

SWING AND AMISS

Chapter 2: Introduction to Position XI, Jazz Swing Cont., Introduction to Jazz Counterpoint

Position XI

Examine position XI and its potential fingerings:

2.1

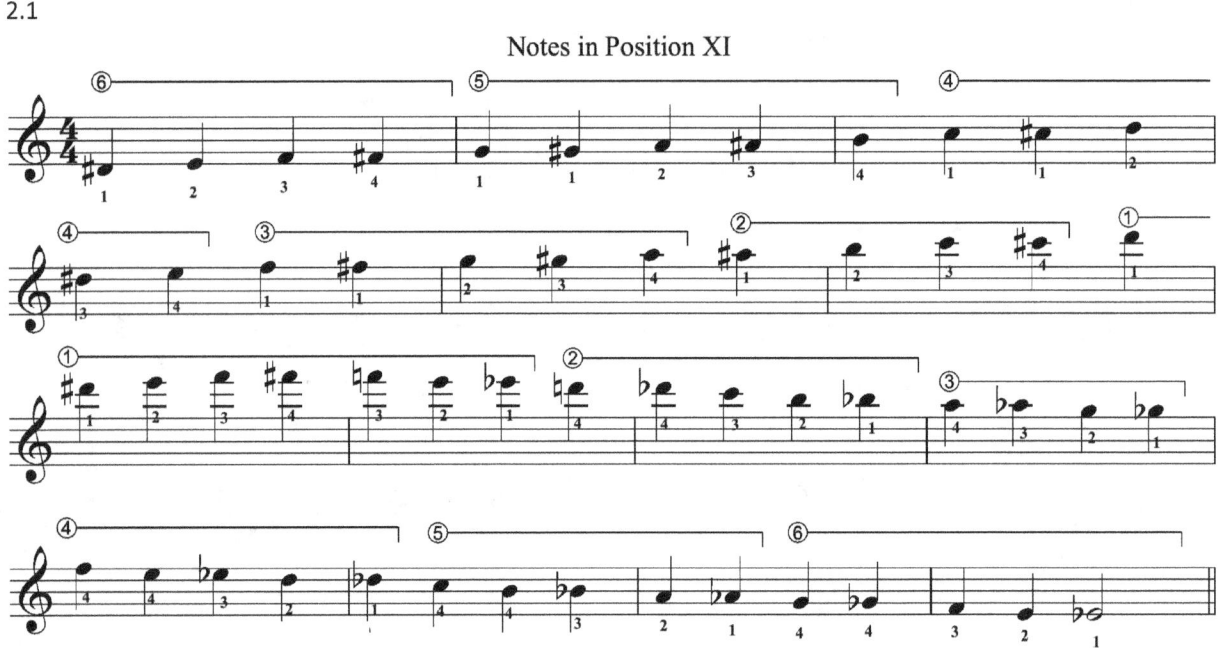

The fingerings here are given in terms of a chromatic scale. It would be perfectly acceptable to use the fingering you find the most comfortable to help construct a good flow for a given musical passage. In the following exercises the fingering choices will be left up to you. Make sure to stay in position XI as you play these passages:

C Major

2.2

2.3

2.4

The exercises below will call upon keys that are ideal for position XI:

E Major

2.4

2.5

2.6

2.7

2.8

C# Minor

2.9

2.10

2.11

2.12

B Major

2.13

2.14

22

2.15

G# Minor

2.16

2.17

2.18

2.19

Jazz Swing Feel Continued

We will now add triplet and 16th note rhythms to our study of jazz swing feel. Triplets would be felt no differently than if they were played straight and 16th notes would remain even although you could still accent the e's and a's a bit stronger. Play the following in any position(s) of your choosing:

2.20

2.21

2.22

2.23

2.24

2.25
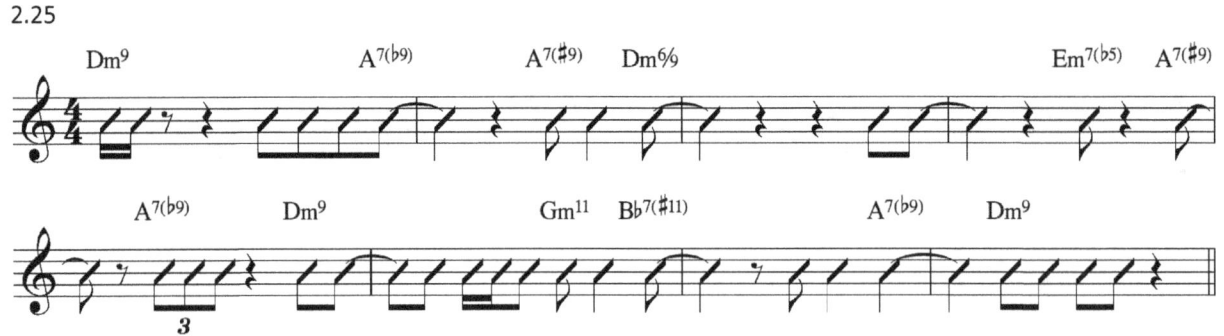

2.26

2.27
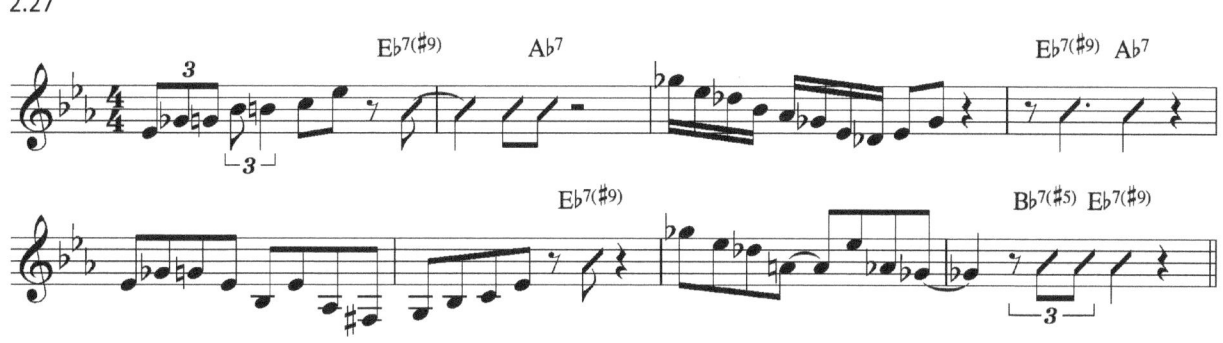

2.28

2.29

2.30

2.31

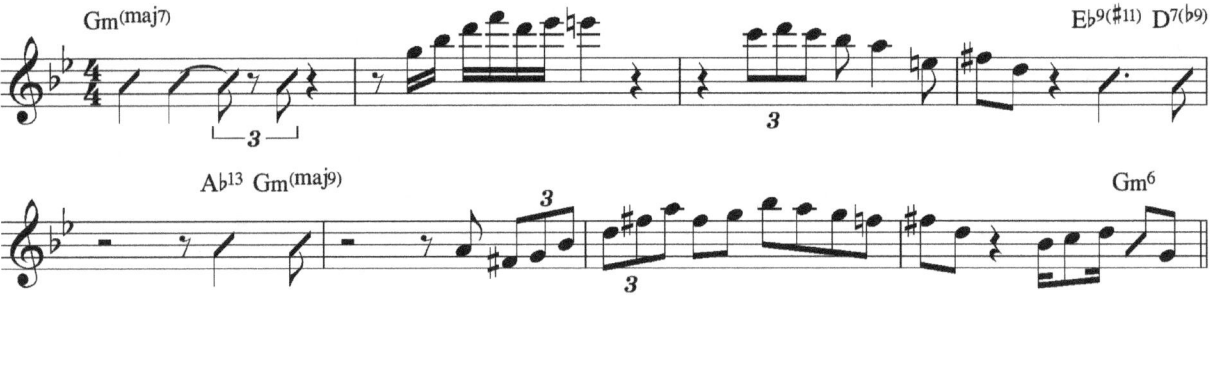

2.32

2.33

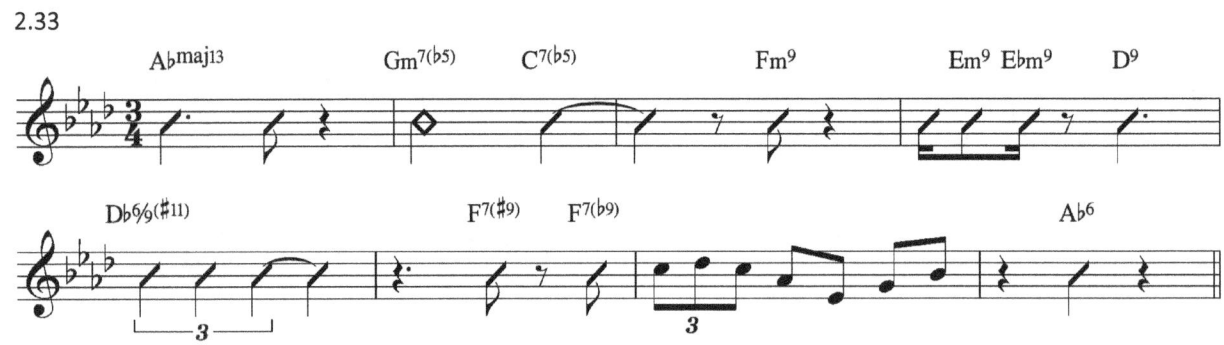

2.34

*The Quadruplet can be found against 3/4 time. It will be four evenly spaced beats in the place of three. The "pull" has a similar effect of a triplet against 4/4 or 2/4 time.

2.35

2.36

2.37

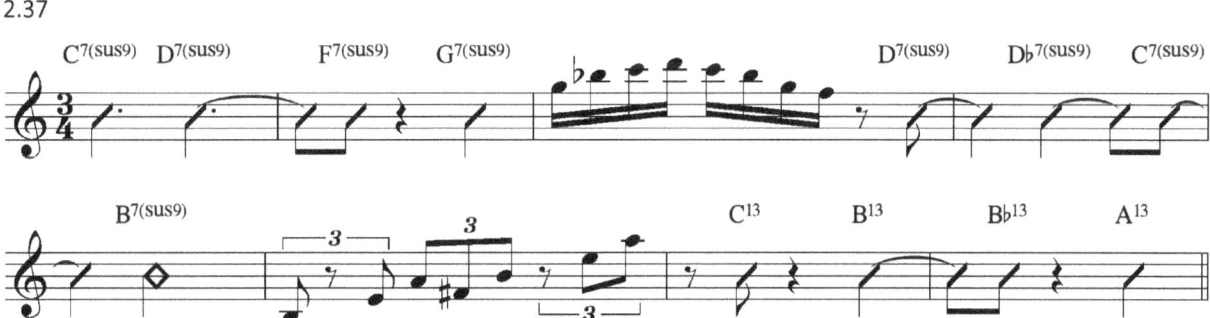

Introduction to Jazz Counterpoint

Jazz counterpoint is often found as chord voicings over walking basslines. It is imperative to let all notes ring out for their full values. You may have to use some unconventional fingerings to allow everything to sound as written. Play the following examples with a swing feel using a combination of open strings and higher positions:

2.42

2.43

Assignment:

Bird's Hit

Chapter 3: Position XI Cont., Jazz Swing Feel Syncopation Cont., and Introduction to Odd Meter

Read the following examples in position XI:

D Major

3.1

3.2

3.3

3.4

3.5

B Minor

3.6

3.7

3.8

3.9

3.10

A Major

3.11

3.12

3.13

3.14

3.15

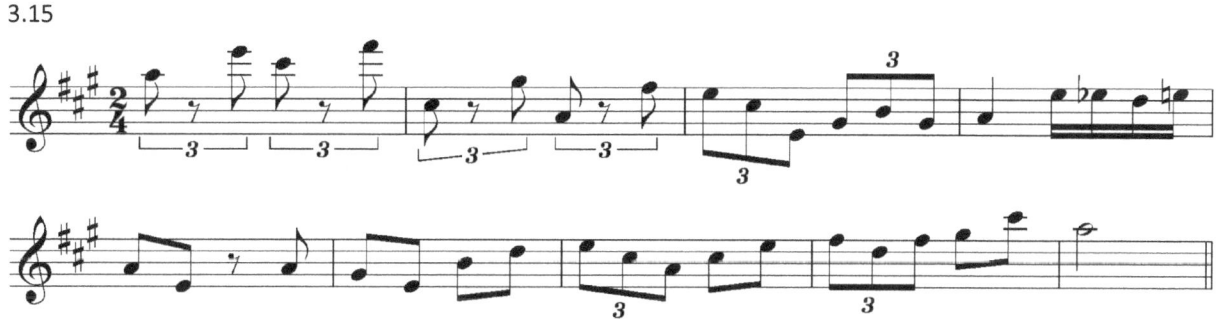

F# Minor

3.16

3.17

3.18

3.19

3.20

Jazz Swing Syncopation Continued

Make sure to swing the 8th notes as you read the following exercises in any position(s):

3.21

3.22

3.27

3.28

*Tremolo- alternate pick note or chord as fast as possible within the confines of the tempo.

3.29

3.30

3.31

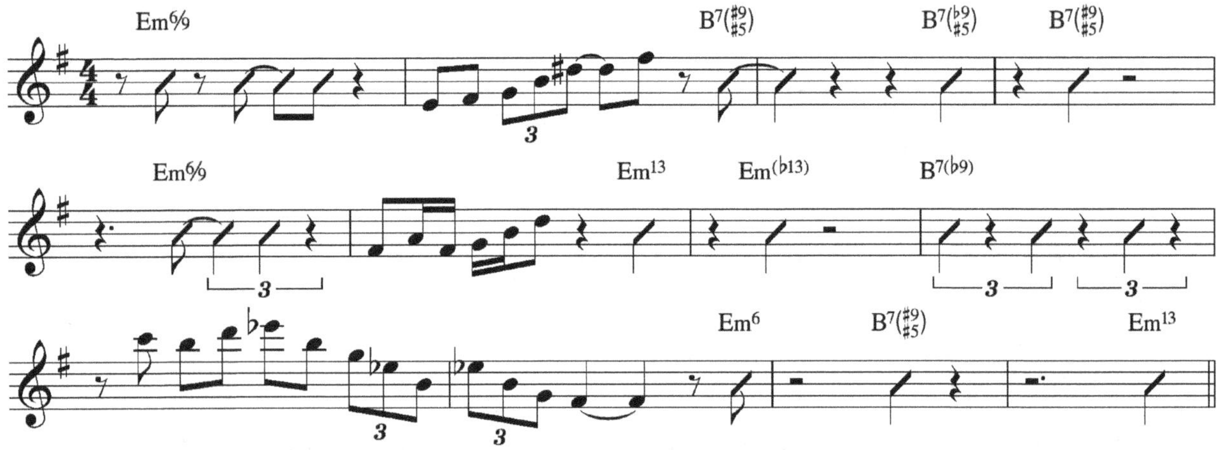
Em6/9
B7(#9 #5)
B7(b9 #5)
B7(#9 #5)
Em6/9
Em13
Em(b13)
B7(b9)
Em6
B7(#9 #5)
Em13

3.32

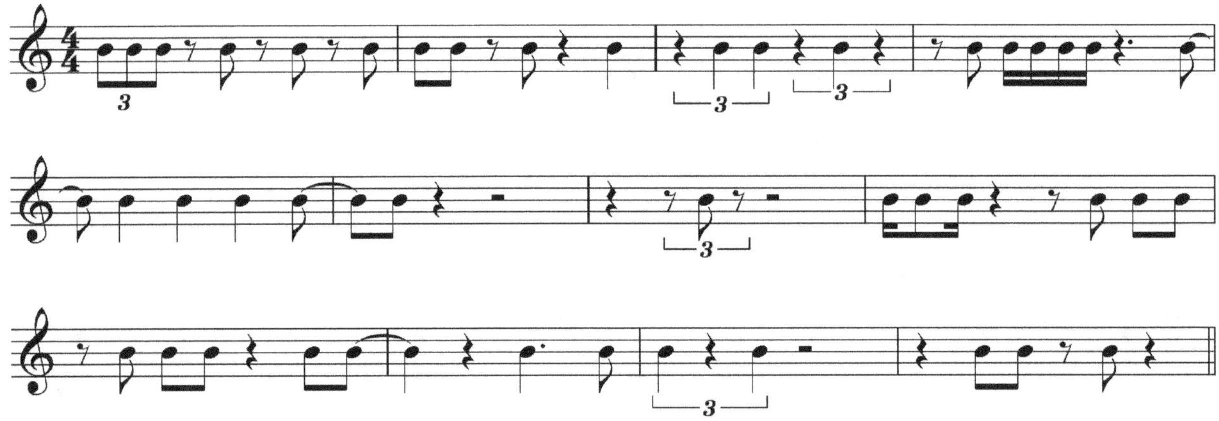

3.33

Bb6/9
Cm7
Bb6/9
Dm7(b5)
G7(#5)
Cm9
F7(b9 #5)
Cm7
F9
Bb6

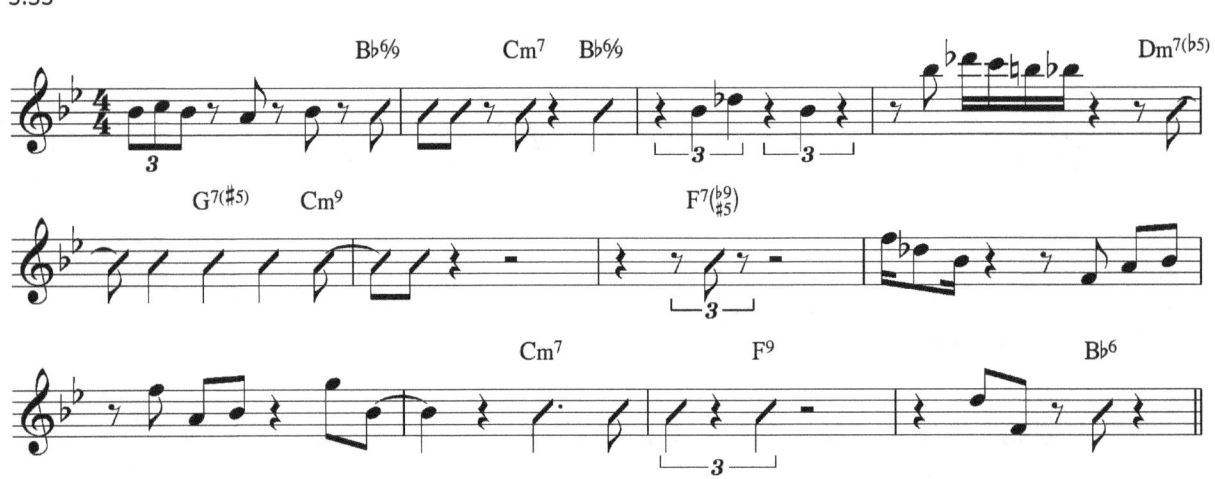

Introduction to Odd Meter

We will begin to study odd meter by examining the 5/4 time signature. Play the following examples in any position(s) you like:

3.34

3.35

3.36

3.37

Assignment:

Chapter 4: Position XI continued, Position X and XI combined, Odd Meter continued. 16th Note Triplets, and Review Exercises

Read the following examples in position XI:

Gb Major

4.1

4.2

Eb Minor

F# Major

D# Minor

4.7

4.8

Combining Positions X and XI

Use positions X and/or XI to create the smoothest fingerings through the following passages:

4.9

4.10

4.11

4.12

4.13

4.14

Odd Meter Continued

Continue to practice odd meter reading with these examples in 7/4. Read in any position(s) you find convenient:

4.15

Try to look for the breakdown of the measure. Is it 4+3 or 3+4? It may be easier to count a bar of 3 and a bar of 4 rather than counting all the way to "seven". Since the word "seven" is two syllables it can be problematic anyways. If you do choose to count all the way to 7, try using the abbreviation "Sev".

4.16

4.17

4.18

52

4.25

4.26

16th Note Triplets

Due to the speed of 16th note triplets it can be difficult to articulate them verbally. Try using a short "t" sound to count out the subdivisions:

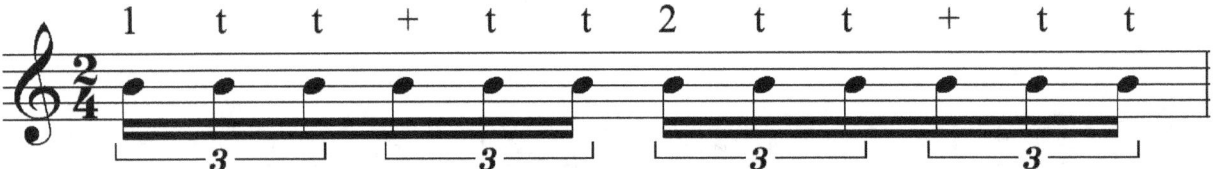

As far as the right hand is concerned, it is best to just alternate picking. 16th note triplets are most commonly consecutive and therefore due to the rate of attacks, the up pick winds up on the "+" as it would with 8th notes.

4.27

4.28

4.29

4.30

4.31

*Oftentimes a 16th note triplet will be part of a line that requires hammer-ons and pull offs. Make sure to play the proper beat divisions before and after the slurs.

**This entire figure is picked only once, on the downbeat of 2.

Cumulative Review Exercises

The following exercises will feature a variety of material covered in previous books combined with some concepts from this one. Pay attention to all details as you perform the examples:

4.35

4.36

4.37

4.42

4.43

Assignment:
Part I: Read in designated positions. Part II: Positions are left to your discretion.

Public Modulation

Chapter 5: Introduction to Position XII, Tied Triplet Syncopation, and Chordal Reading in Position VII

Position XII

Examine position XII and its potential fingerings:

5.1

The fingerings here are given in terms of a chromatic scale. As before, it would be perfectly acceptable to use the fingering you find the most comfortable to help construct a good flow for a given musical passage. Make sure to stay in position XII as you play these passages:

C Major

5.2

A Minor

F Major

5.15

5.16

D Minor

5.17

5.18

5.19

5.20

5.21

Tied Eighth Note Triplet Syncopation Swing Exercises

The following rhythmic examples feature tied eighth note triplet rhythms. Perform them until comfortable using the pick directions established in earlier units. The second example of each pair which will feature identical rhythms with moving pitches. Choose the position that best matches the range and key. ALL exercises swing:

5.30

5.31

Jazz Chordal Reading Position VII

Use your knowledge of how to visualize intervals on the staff as you try to read these four and five-part chord voicings in position VII:

5.32

5.33

5.34

5.35

5.36

5.37

5.38

5.39

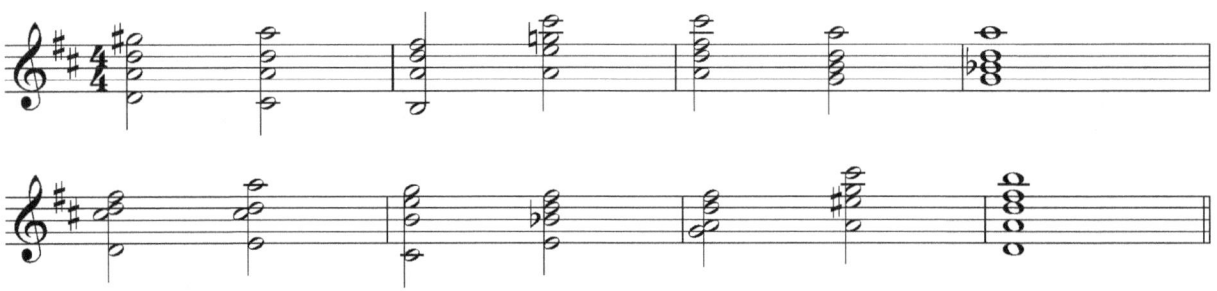

5.40

This page has been intentionally left blank

Assignment:

Calypso Collapse-O

Chapter 6: Position XII Cont., Chordal Reading in Position IX, Introduction to Mixed Meter, 32nd note reading

Play the following exercises in position XII:

G Major

6.8

6.9

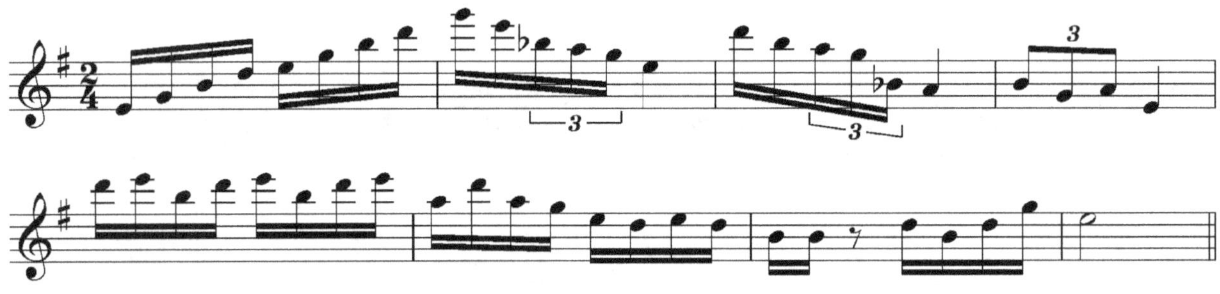

6.10

Chordal Reading Position IX

Read these four-part chord voicings in position IX:

6.11

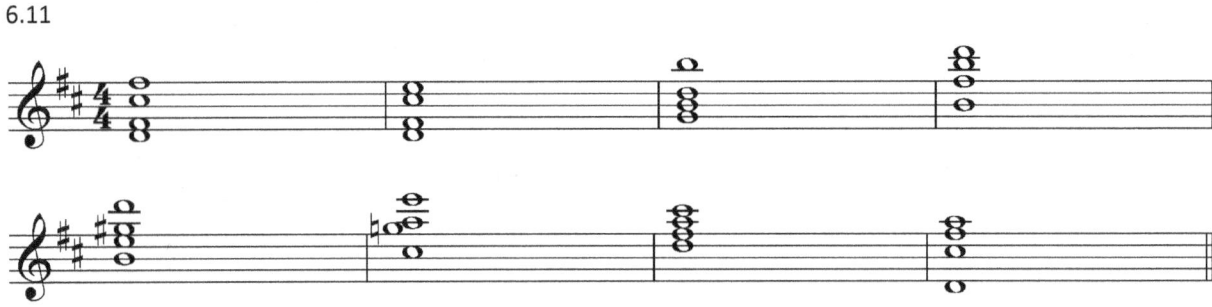

Mixed Meter

We will begin our study of mixed meter with exercises that share a denominator. In these situations, you will need to adjust to the changing number of beats in each measure. Make sure to keep track of beat 1 as you read the following exercises in any position(s) of your choosing:

6.17

6.18

6.19

*In these measures of 5/8 think about picking Down-Up-Down-Down-Up as your subdivision so it feels like a bar of 3/8 + 2/8.

6.23

6.24

6.25

6.26

83

6.27

6.28

6.29

6.30

6.31

6.32

32nd Note Reading

32nd notes are rare at most tempos due to how fast they can be. But you might encounter them at slower speeds. Interpret and pick them as follows:

6.33

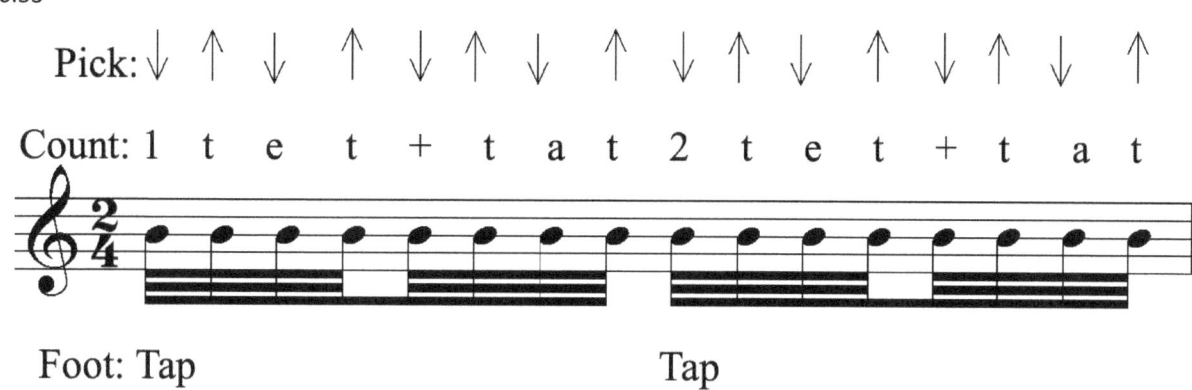

If the rhythm's become more complex, it may be easier to count with the same subdivisions that you might use for 16th notes (1 e + a). Just keep track of where the down beats are.

6.34

Play the following exercises in any position(s) you choose:

6.35

6.40

6.41

6.42

6.43

6.44

This page has been intentionally left blank

Assignment:

Kermit The Prog

Chapter 7: Position XII Cont., Mixed Meter Cont., Comprehensive Review Exercises

Play the following exercises in position XII:

Eb Major

7.1

7.2

7.3

7.4

7.5

C Minor

7.6

7.7

7.8

7.9

7.10

Position VII 8va Review

Read the following exercises and octave higher than written in position VII:

7.11

7.12

7.13

7.14

7.15

Position X 8va Review

Read the following exercises and octave higher than written in position X:

7.16

7.17

7.18

7.19

7.20

Mixed Meter Continued

In this chapter we will study mixed meter with a varying denominator. The most common variation would be shifting between /4 and /8. There are three common ways the variance in meter could be interpreted. Here they are in order from MOST to LEAST common:

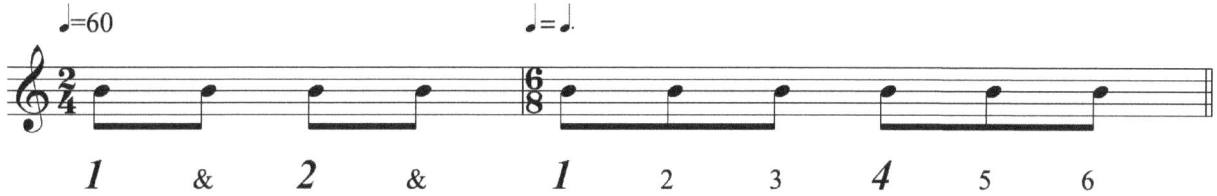

The beats in italics represent where your metronome would be clicking at a tempo of 60 BPM. When the quarter note in /4 equals a dotted quarter note in /8, the 8th note counts will be slightly faster (feeling just like 8th note triplets in /4).

The simplest way to transition between changing denominators is to break down the metronome to the Lowest Common Denominator. In the above situation the metronome speed has been doubled so that in the 2/4 measure and the 6/8 measure the 8th note remains constant and will be played each time the metronome clicks. The overall tempo is no faster than the previous example, but the metronome is now subdividing the quarter note. There is no change in speed when the 6/8 measure occurs, the change is in the interpretation of the count only. The 8th notes in 6/8 are played at the same speed as the 8th notes in 2/4.

In the above situation, the quarter note of the 2/4 and the 8th note of the 6/8 would be felt at an identical speed. This means the 6/8 would feel much slower than the 2/4.

There are other possibilities in metric modulation but understanding these scenarios should help you figure out any others you encounter.

Play the following examples three times each. Each time use a different one of the three modulation concepts detailed above (or their inversions depending on the initial meter):

7.21

7.22

7.23

7.24

7.25

7.26

7.27

7.28

7.29

7.30

7.31

Articulation Review Exercises

Read the following examples using positions X-XII. Focus on executing the written articulations:

7.32

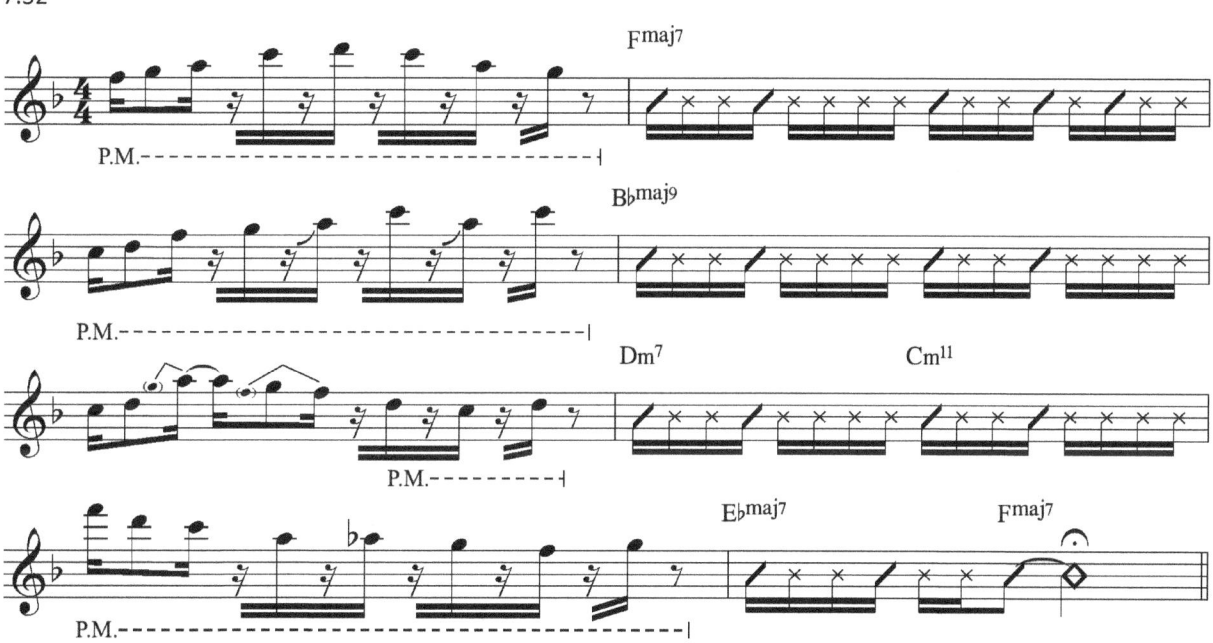

7.33

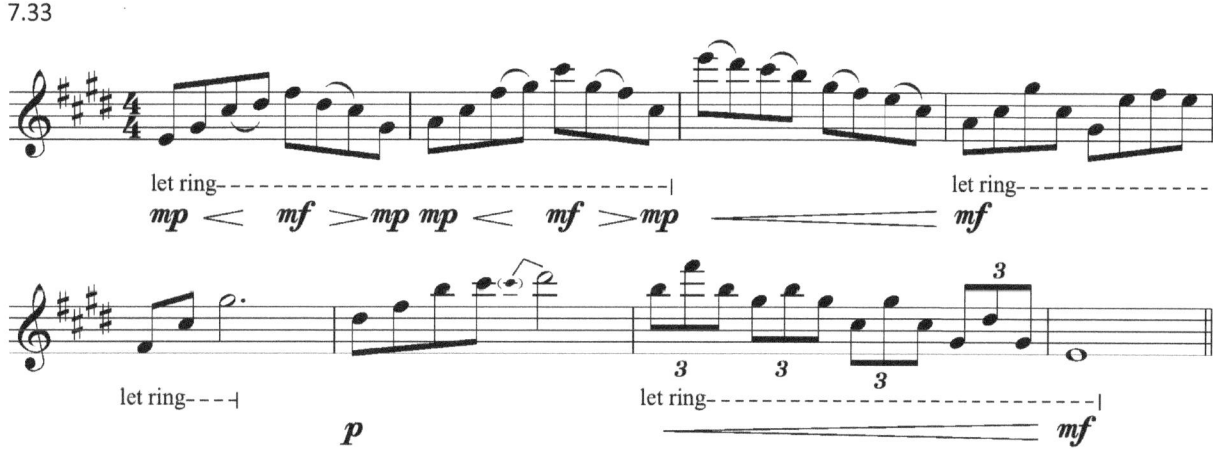

7.34

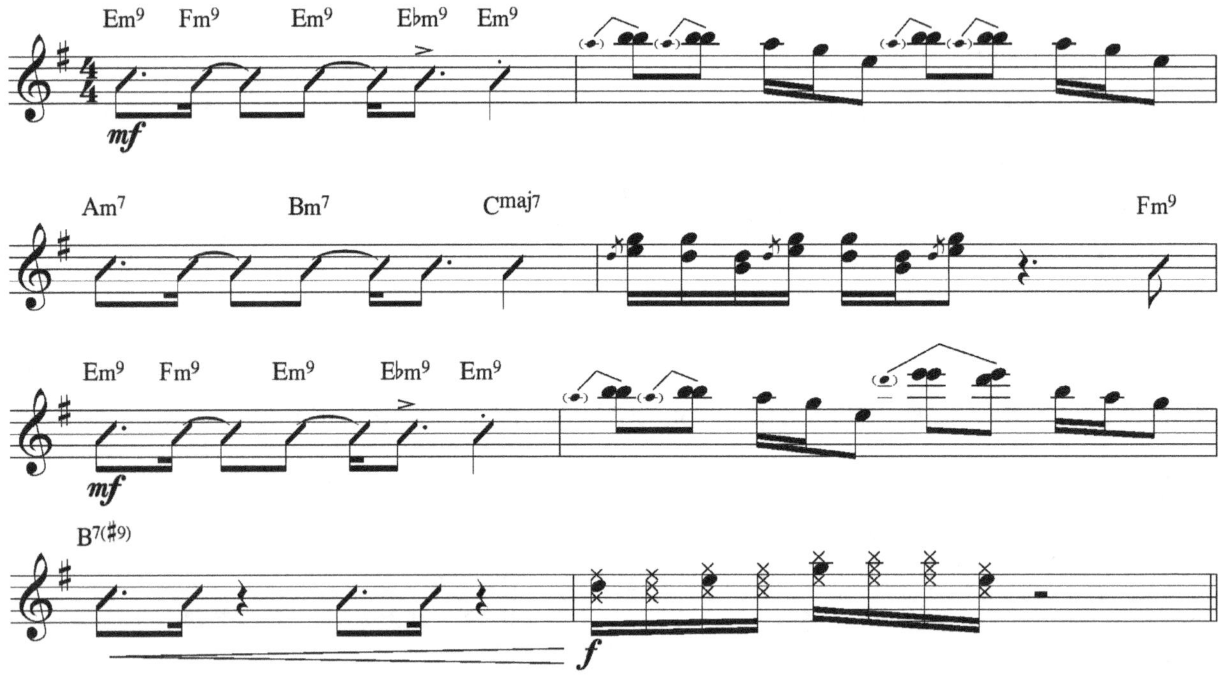
Em9 Fm9 Em9 E♭m9 Em9
mf
Am7 Bm7 Cmaj7 Fm9
Em9 Fm9 Em9 E♭m9 Em9
mf
B7(♯9)
f

7.35

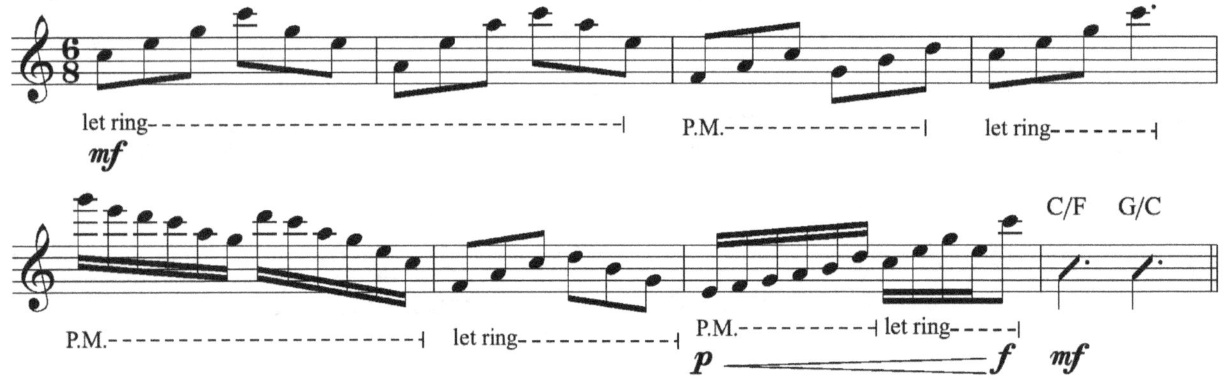
let ring
mf
P.M.
let ring
P.M.
let ring
P.M.
let ring
p
f
C/F G/C
mf

7.36

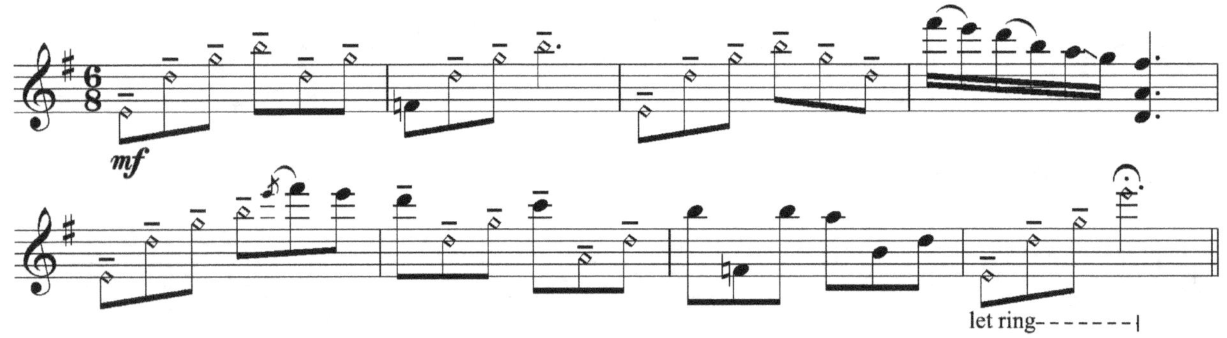
mf
let ring

7.37

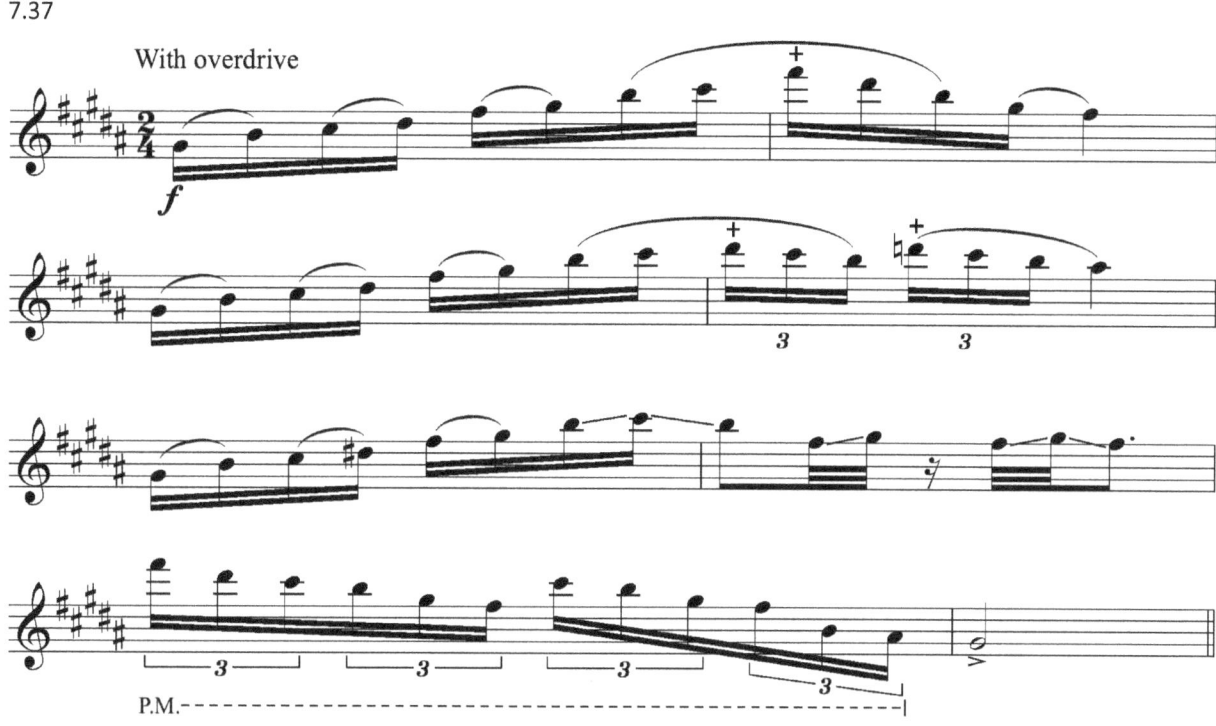

Assignment:

Dynamic Duo

Music only found in a Guitar Reading Book ♩ = 65

Chapter 8: Introduction to Position XII 8va, Double and Triple stops in Position IX, Jazz Syncopation and Odd Meter Review

Play the following examples in Position XII and octave higher than written:

C Major

8.1

8.2

A Minor

8.3

8.4

F Major

8.5

8.6

D Minor

8.7

8.8

G Major

8.9

8.10

E Minor

8.11

8.12

Bb Major

8.13

8.14
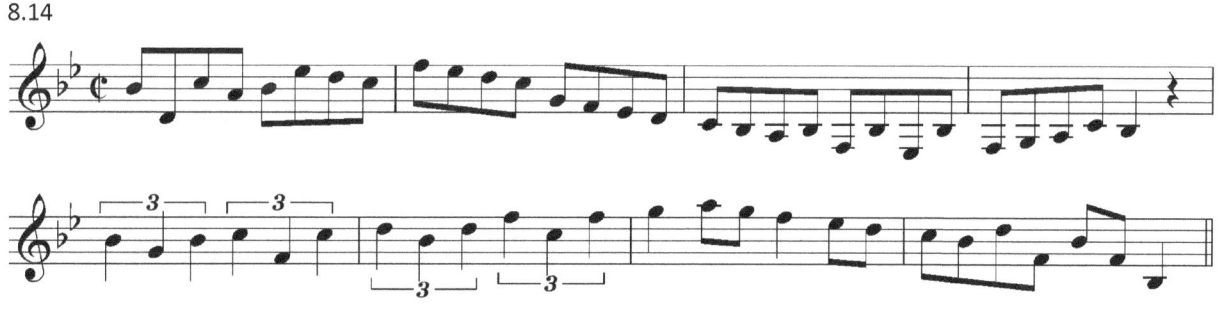

G Minor

8.15

8.16

8.17

Eb Major

8.18

C Minor

8.19

Jazz Syncopation Review Exercises

Play the following swung 8th note examples in any position(s) you see fit:

8.20

8.21

8.22

8.23

8.24

8.25

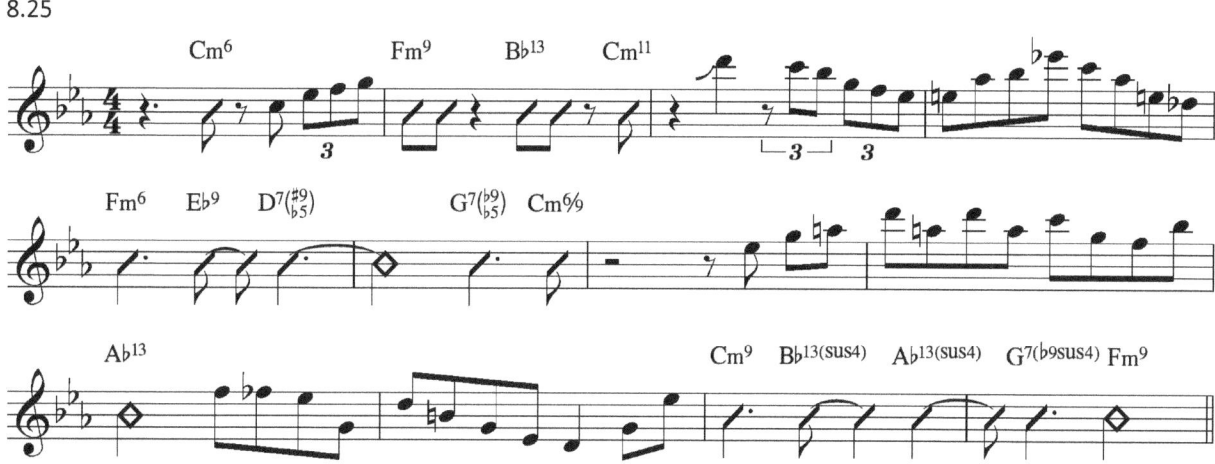

Double and Triple Stop Reading

Play the following examples in position IX:

8.26

8.27

8.28

8.29

8.30

8.31

8.32

Odd Meter Reading Review

Read the following example in any position(s) you choose:

8.33

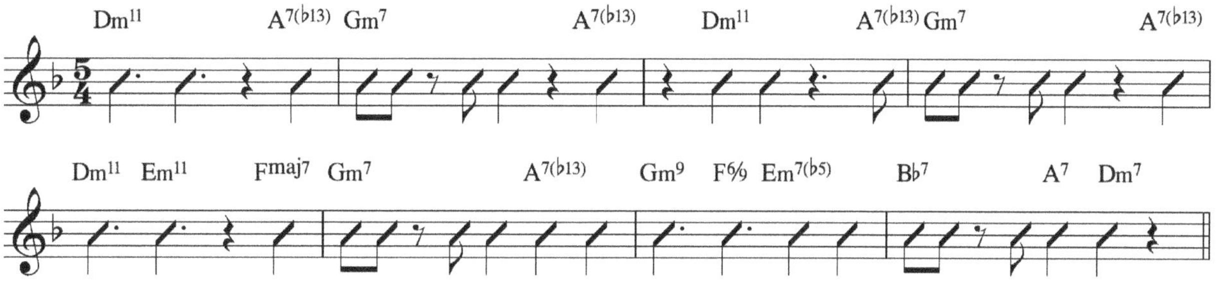

8.34

8.35

8.36

8.37

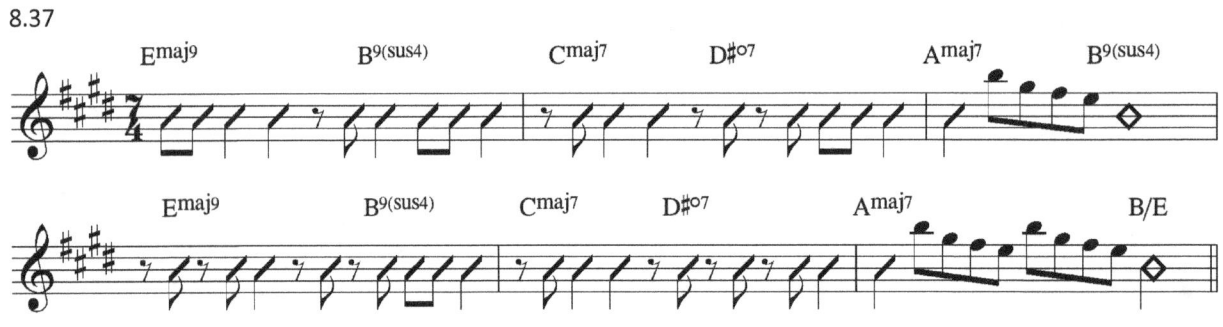

8.38

8.39

8.40

Assignment:

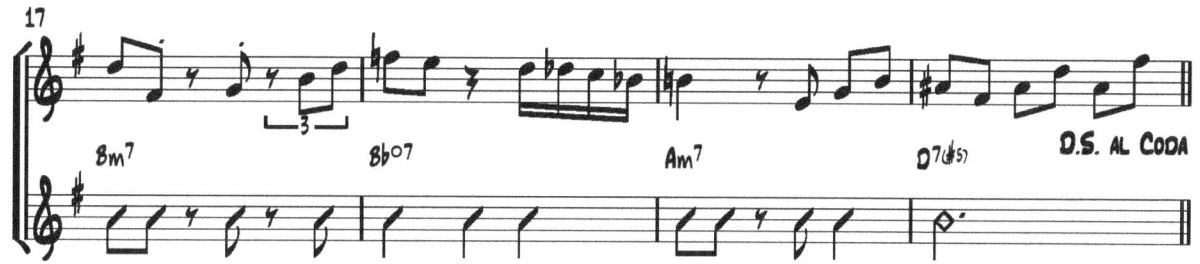
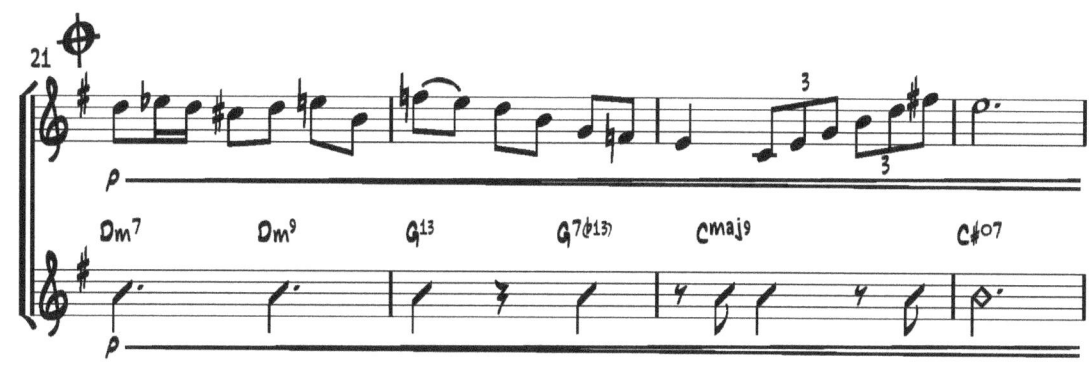

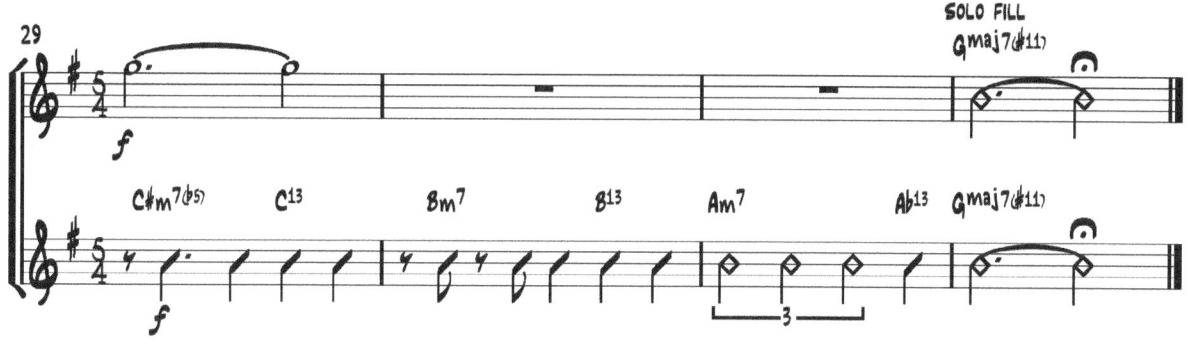

Chapter 9: High Register Reading, Double Stop Reading (Horizontal Approach, and Mixed Meter Review Exercises

Interpret previously learned positions twelve frets higher as you play the following exercises an octave higher than written (you are allowed to shift positions as you play):

9.1

9.2

9.3

*Some guitars may not have this note on the 22nd fret. Try not to feel inadequate if your guitar only has 21 frets.

9.8

9.9

9.10

High Ledger Line Reading

Although not as common as reading 8va, there will be times when it may be necessary to recognize the higher register of the guitar *as written*. Here are the notes on the staff from the 15th fret of the 1st string and above:

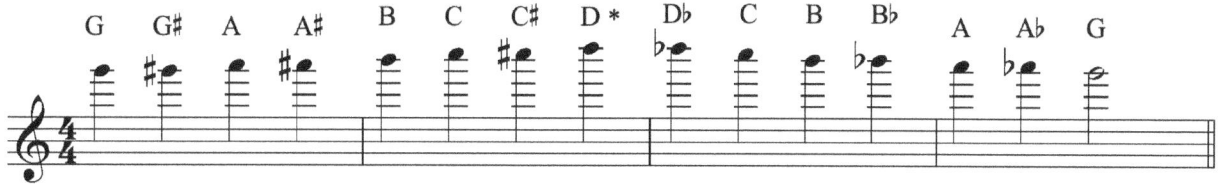

*As previously mentioned, this D would be the 22nd fret of the 1st string, which not all guitars may have. Some guitars may continue up to 24 frets, but if you purchased one of those, you probably did not intend to do any reading on it anyways!

Read the following examples in any position(s) you choose:

9.11

9.12

9.13

9.14
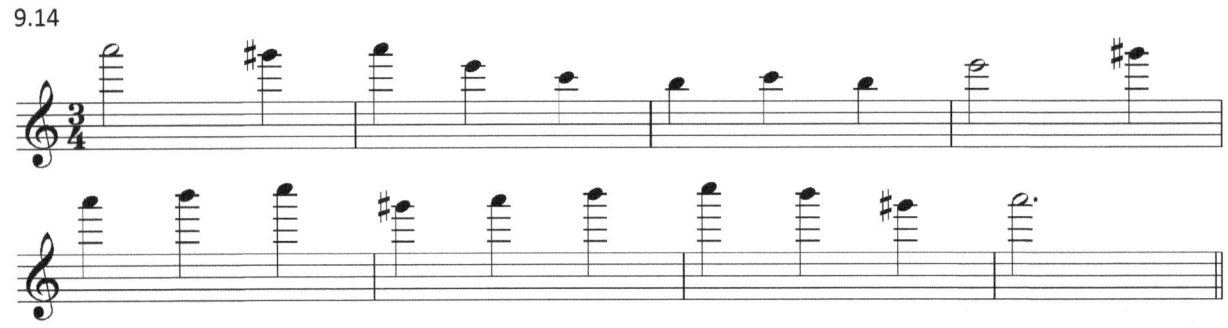

9.15

9.16
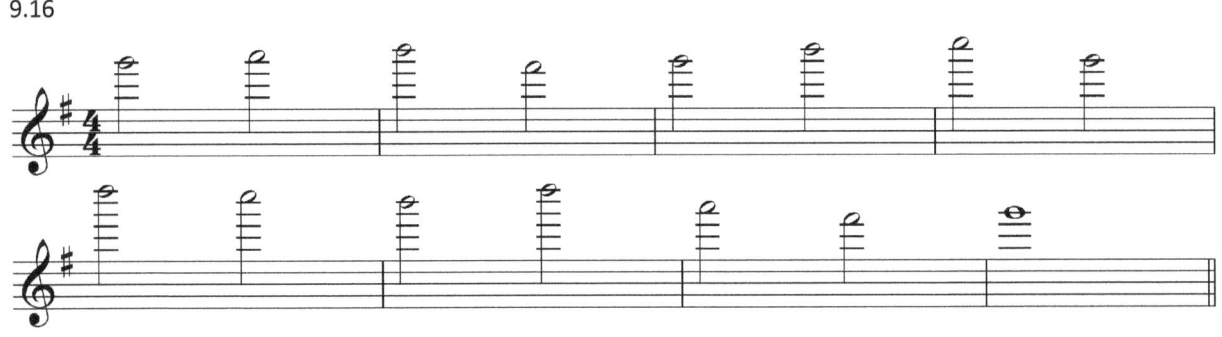

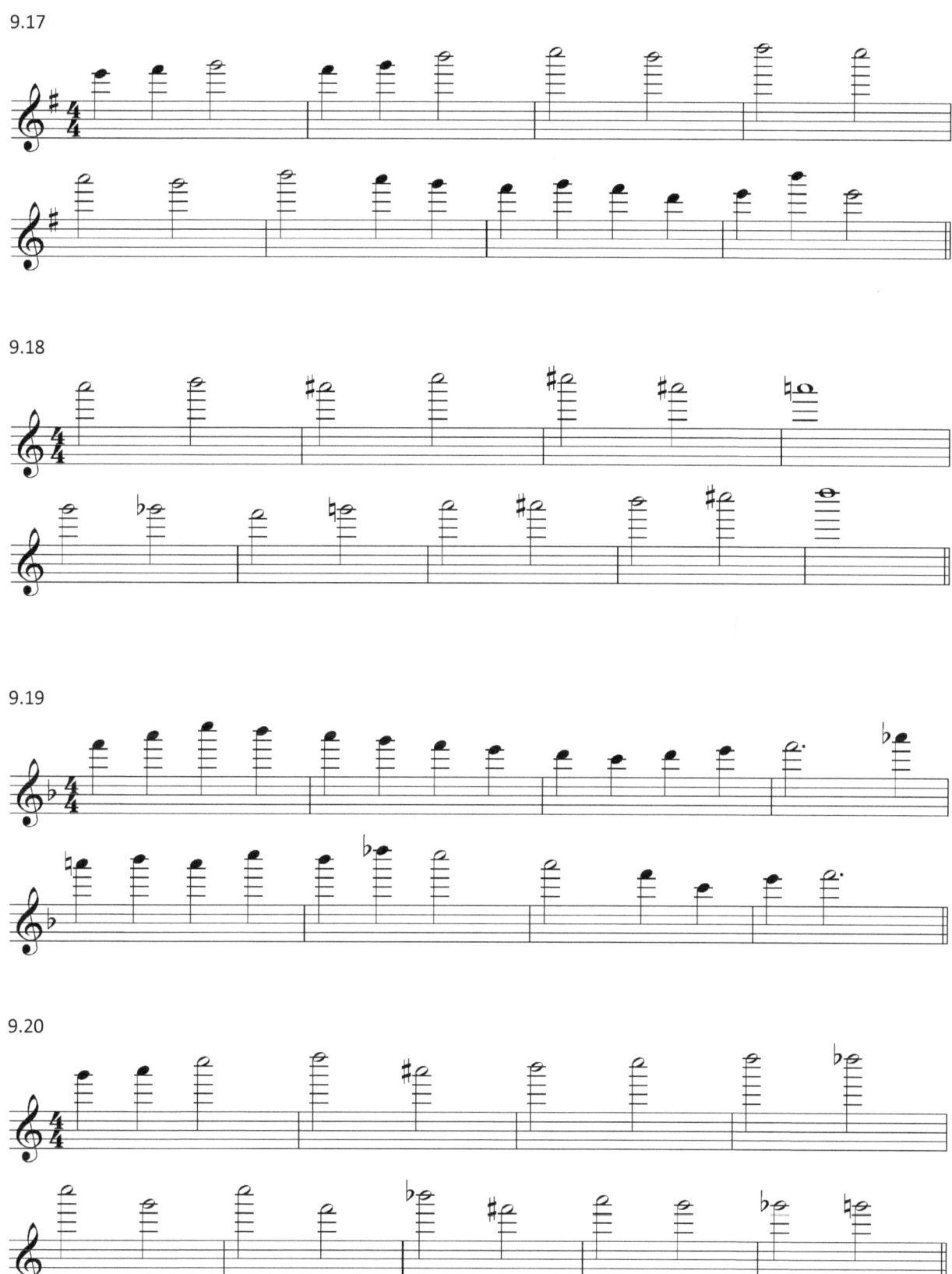

Double Stop Reading: Horizontal Approach

Oftentimes it is easier to perform parallel double stops by moving up and down the fretboard, rather than across. In the following examples, freely change positions if you encounter parallel double stops:

9.21

9.22

9.23

9.24

9.25

9.26

9.27

9.28

9.29

9.30

Mixed Meter Review Exercises

Play the following examples three times each in any position(s) you choose. Each time use a different one of the three modulation concepts (or their inversions depending on the initial meter):

Assignment:

Chapter 10: Positions I-XII Combined, Harmony Reading (Horizontal Approach), Odd and Mixed Meter Applied Reading

Positionless Reading

The result of familiarizing yourself with all the positions on the guitar neck is to be able to look at a given series of pitches and identify the most convenient area to play them. Look for the range of a passage, the key, and where the fingering sits without an excess amount of stretching or awkward fingerings when identifying the *position of the moment*. Switch positions as many times as necessary to accommodate this. Use rests, open strings, or longer note holds to facilitate switches. Eventually you should be able to shift even during a fluid series of notes as you get more comfortable with the process. The following exercises will contain wide range reading and from here on, all position choices will be left up to you:

10.1

10.2

10.3

10.4

10.5

10.6

10.7

10.8

10.9

10.10

10.11

10.12

10.13

10.14

10.15

10.16

10.17

10.18

10.19

Harmony Reading (Horizontal Approach)

Try to move up and down the neck in a parallel manner on these exercises:

10.20

10.21

10.22

10.27

10.28

10.29

10.30

Odd and Mixed Meter Review Exercises

Read the following examples using any position(s) you choose:

10.31

10.32

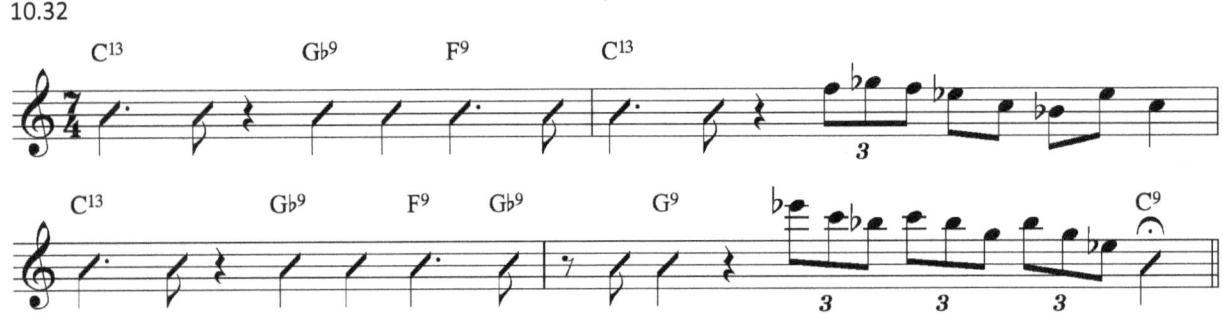

10.33

10.34

10.35

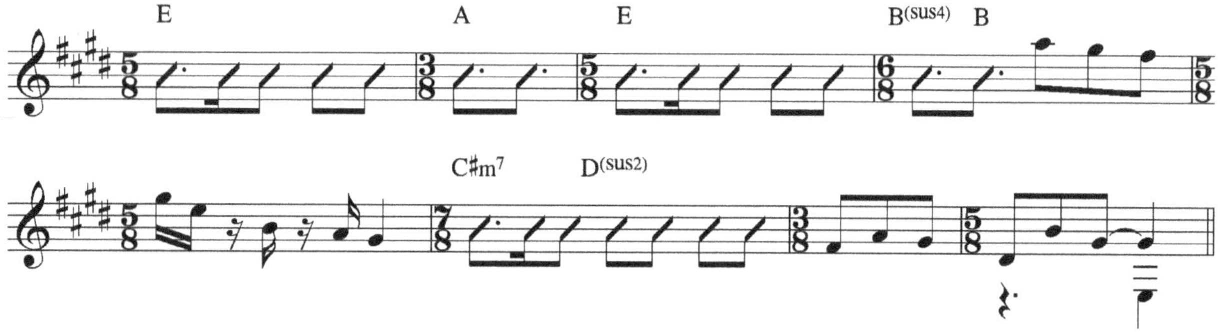

10.36

10.37

Practice Charts

Pro Fusion Confusion

Passical Gas

About the Author

Ian Robbins graduated from USC with a Bachelor's and Master's degree in Studio/Jazz performance. He has had airplay on KJAZ 88.1FM and other national jazz stations as a member of the Bruce Escovitz Jazz Orchestra (BEJO). He recorded on BEJO's 2008 Album Invitation. Invitation spent several weeks in the top half of the Billboard Jazz charts. Ian recently recorded Guitar, Ukulele, and Mandolin tracks for a song used for a promotional video for the NBC TV Show *This Is Us* and for a movie trailer for *I Love You Berlin,* which starred Helen Mirren and Kira Knightly. Ian has performed with Landau Eugene Murphy Jr.- The winner of NBC's *America's Got Talent* Season 6. Ian has previously performed/recorded with Barry Manilow, Bonnie Raitt, Wynton Marsalis, Peter Erskine, Toni Tennille, Louis Bellson, Ndugu Chancellor, Stu Hamm, Kurt Elling, Ernie Watts, Marilyn McCoo, Alan Chang, Scott Henderson, and many others. Ian has also done session work for Grammy winning producer Bobby Watson and for Nickelodeon Studios. Recently Ian recorded for the JGAH project in Korea (arranged by Dr. Rachel Yoon), a Korean traditional music group that has performed live over 200 times along to Ian's prerecorded fusion guitar tracks.

Ian is currently on the faculty at Musician's Institute. As part of the Bachelor Degree Program he teaches Guitar Technique, Guitar Reading, Songwriting, Performance classes in Punk, Blues Rock and Fusion (the latter with former co/teacher Russell Ferrante), Ear Training, Private Lessons and Open Counseling. He also teaches the KPOP, Zawinul and Coffee House International LPWs. Ian has traveled, performed, and taught in Asia several times as part of MI's outreach program.

Ian Robbins is also the lead guitarist/singer/songwriter of original punk rock band Get Out™. Get Out™ has released 8 albums, which have sold on 6 continents and performed hundreds of shows. Get Out™'s YouTube channel currently has over 40,000 views (none of which were purchased). They have been endorsed by energy drink company Nitro 2 Go and have gotten airplay on various local stations. The band has performed on LA18 television and has shared the stage with such national acts as Voodoo Glow Skulls, Streetlight Manifesto, MXPX, and Suburban Legends. In January 2015, Get Out™ released *Epilogue* with the help of drummer Jeff Bowders (Paul Gilbert, Shakira). *Epilogue* is a 19 minute progressive punk rock epic currently being sold on iTunes and other online distributors. Get Out™ released their 8th album *The Violations of Terms and Conditions* in 2022.

Ian is a member of Hip Hop/Electronica group Dancing Mischief, which has received airplay on KCRW FM.

Ian also plays guitar for Korean Grammy winning artist Ann One. Ann One has performed at KCON 2018, the Korean Society of Maryland's annual festival, on LA18's Halo Halo, and was featured on the pilot episode of the Asian American web series *Sessions at Studio 5A*.

Ian Robbins has published a book entitled *Beginning Guitar for the Songwriter* available online as both a print book and an ebook.

www.ingramcontent.com/pod-product-compliance
Lightning Source LLC
Chambersburg PA
CBHW081154070526
44583CB00021B/2832